Copyright

Copyright © 2019 by Dr. Jennifer Cooper Scott

Published by Dr. Jennifer Cooper Scott

ISBN 978-0-359-91819-5

All rights reserved. This book or any portion thereof may not be reproduced or used in any manner whatsoever without the express written permission of the publisher except for the use of brief quotations in a book review or scholarly journal.

Disclaimer

Although the author and publisher have made every effort to ensure that the information in this book was correct at press time, the author and publisher do not assume and hereby disclaim any liability to any party for any loss, damage, or disruption caused by errors or omissions, whether such errors or omissions result from negligence, accident, or any other cause.

Connect with the Author

Email: Jennifer.cooper@alumni.twu.edu

LinkedIn Profile: https://www.linkedin.com/in/jennifer-cooper-scott-edd-91a512134/

Contents

Acknowledgements

About the Author

Introduction

Chapter 1 – What is Anxiety

Chapter 2 – Anxiety vs. Panic Attacks

Chapter 3 – Physical Effects of Anxiety on the Body

Chapter 4 – Understanding Anxiety – A Teacher's Perspective

Chapter 5 – Trauma in the Classroom

Chapter 6 – Self-Care During Periods of Anxiety

Chapter 7 – How to Cope with Anxiety

Acknowledgements

I wanted to thank everyone that took the time to assist me with this endeavor! The multitude of family, friends, and colleagues that provided support and encouragement in writing this book is priceless. I also want to thank the educators that took the time out to speak to me and share their experiences.

About the Author

Dr. Jennifer Cooper Scott is an enthusiastic, dynamic, and dedicated educator with over five years of experience as a Special Education Teacher. She is passionate and committed to safeguarding and advocating for the education and well-being of students at all levels as well as advocating and mentoring teachers. Her expertise provides a track record of excellent curriculum/course design and development and the facilitation of exemplary instruction to students of varying backgrounds and learning needs. She is an expert in the fields of special education, organizational leadership, and teacher burnout. Dr. Scott brings exceptional interpersonal and intrapersonal skills with a wealth of experience building partnerships with colleagues, parents, and scholars.

Introduction

Anxiety affects 6.8 million people a year and it is a constant struggle for teachers. This book goes into deep detail of the binding nature of anxiety from the teacher's perspective. To bring to light the taboo subject of anxiety among educators, I interviewed several teachers about their experiences and how they cope with anxiety on a daily basis. I also wanted to share my experience, so I included my own battle with anxiety that increased significantly from a traumatic experience in the classroom and how I overcame it. The book offers information to assist you in understanding anxiety, provides self-care techniques and coping strategies to support you in working through the anxiety, and a list of resources that you can contact if you need additional assistance. I am not a medical doctor, only sharing personal knowledge I have learned during my own experiences with anxiety.

Chapter 1 – What is Anxiety

First, let's discuss what the definition of anxiety is. The Webster dictionary has two different definitions of anxiety. The one I want to focus on is the medical definition they have listed. They state that anxiety is an abnormal and overwhelming sense of apprehension and fear. This sense is often marked by physical signs such as tension, sweating, increased pulse rate, and self-doubt about one's capacity to cope with it (Webster, 2019). When I looked up anxiety to see how to define it there were so many definitions; uneasiness, fear, being apprehensive, doubt, and mentally distressing. I believe that anxiety, depending on what you are going through, encompasses all of these definitions at one point or another. For me, this anxiety didn't settle in until much later in life as I started my first year teaching special education. I had no idea where it came from, how I got it or even what to do about it.

I've spoken to other educators who have defined anxiety in other ways such as a feeling of being overwhelmed, excessive crying, and those that have suffered physical ailments. Anxiety can be debilitating in life and can be harmful if not treated by the proper doctor. I was inspired to write this book to not only help other educators that are currently experiencing bouts of anxiety but to shed light on the issue of anxiety in teaching. I also wanted to shed light on how you can assist an educator going through anxiety without them feeling judged. It is not easy for someone to admit that they have anxiety and it is not easy for them to seek help. So be kind, patient, and understanding to those people around you that are experiencing anxiety.

I couldn't find the exact number of educators that suffer from anxiety but did see that 6.8 million American adults suffer from an anxiety disorder. I often wonder out of that 6.8 million, how many are educators? What are we doing to assist our teachers through anxiety, self-care, and how to maintain a sense of self-worth during these challenging times?

On a personal note, anxiety looked much like what the Webster dictionary described it as, uneasiness, fear, being apprehensive, doubt, and mentally distressing. It hit me as I was sitting at a red light on my way to eat lunch with a couple of friends. It progressed slowly starting as burning at the bottom of my feet working its way up to tightness in my chest. By the time I reached the restaurant,

I had to turn around and leave. I couldn't breathe, I couldn't stop shaking, and I couldn't stop crying. What was causing this? Why now? What was I doing or thinking about that would make me so anxious? My friend followed me home that day and stopped and got me something to eat and drink. I slept for a good four-plus hours after that episode. I never had an anxiety attack before. Was it an anxiety attack? Was it a panic attack? Is there a difference between the two? I had to find out for sure what this was, what was causing them, and how I could help myself through it.

Anxiety is fear, uneasiness, doubt, stress, worry, headaches, and can be described in many other ways. Anxiety can be debilitating, it can run your life, it can cause you to become lonely, and it can ruin your life if you let it. Anxiety can be extreme, or it can be mild. It can cause you to have insomnia or a lack of appetite and suddenly you become nauseated. Anxiety can be many things, but it does not mean you are less of a person, less of a teacher, and it does not mean you are not worthy! YOU MATTER!

Chapter 2 – Anxiety vs. Panic Attacks

Now that we have discussed what anxiety is, let's dive deeper into the differences between anxiety and panic attacks from a personal perspective. Let me preface this by saying again that I am not a medical doctor, all the information I am presenting in these chapters are either from personal experience or from some amount of research that has been done. I personally have experienced both anxiety and a panic attack and let me tell you they are different!

First, anxiety slowly approaches you like a thief in the night and then suddenly you realize you have it. For me, the physical effects of anxiety start at the bottom of my feet like a burning sensation and then works its way up to my chest and shoulders. This is normally a slower process and I can feel it coming on. This anxiety can last minutes, hours or even for the whole day depending on the situation. I have been told that anxiety depends on the situation you are in and can often be remedied by removing yourself from the situation. But I believe that anxiety is also when you get to overthinking things, when you dwell on circumstances and situations, and when you become so exhausted due to your situation that your mind races a million miles a minute. I once had an anxiety attack right before an IEP meeting. This was a student that I had not worked with, I didn't have in my class, and the parent was very agitated with the situation. I wasn't sure how this meeting was going to end or how it was even going to work out. So, in my mind, I got worked up and the anxiety set in throughout the day because of course the IEP meeting was set for the afternoon. I couldn't excuse myself from the meeting, I was the special education teacher representative! Everyone was looking at me while I was discussing the information in the PLAAFP. The anxiety lasted throughout the whole meeting and I had to remind myself that I was ok. It was situational, it was able to be controlled, and I made it through the meeting. Everyone is different and your anxiety may be triggered by different things, in different ways, and for different reasons. Whatever your version of anxiety is, there is a way to work through it, but we will get to that in a later chapter.

Second, panic attacks are all the sudden! There is no precursor to these in my personal experience. All of the sudden you find yourself in a state of panic. One time I had a complete panic attack on the floor in the Las Vegas airport. It was all of the sudden and I was in a complete panic as I was on the floor digging through my purse looking for the money, I brought to Vegas to spend. It was a lot and I can't believe that I lost it! It was gone! I had no idea what happened to it as I had just gotten off a three-hour flight! Where did it go? Who took it? I was in tears sitting on the floor screaming where did it go. My friend who was with me couldn't help; she didn't know what to do! Come to find out my husband had it the whole time and all was well. But I remember the feeling of that sudden panic attack and then came the embarrassment of sitting on the floor in a public place crying, screaming, and in a complete panic. My heart was pounding what felt like a million miles a minute. I was hot all the sudden. I couldn't breathe. People were staring at me. It was sudden and then it was gone but the physical effects lasted throughout the day. I was tired, I was embarrassed, I was cranky, and I didn't know how to fix it in the future. For me, there was a reason for this panic attack but for many, there may not be a visible reason.

Panic attacks just like anxiety attacks can vary in how they look and how intense they are depending on the person. Can panic and anxiety be triggered by the same things, sure they can! Can they work simultaneously, sure they can. Can you have one without the other or have both, yes you sure can! The important thing to know and learn is how to help a person when they are experiencing a panic or anxiety attack! It is important as a mentor, an administrator, a friend, and an educator to know what anxiety looks like, what a panic attack looks like, and how it affects a person going through them. It is also important not to judge them during the attack or after. Remember we are all human but some deal with stress and situations differently than others.

Chapter 3 – Physical Effects of Anxiety on the Body

We do not always realize the physical effects of anxiety on our bodies and what that looks like. I've spoken to many current and previous teachers that describe what they are going through as just tired or exhausted. But they do not realize exactly what those physical effects are. That exhaustion turns into a cold, the flu, physical aches and pains, migraines, and a variety of other physical attributes that affect the body. In my previous book, I discussed self-care and what that looks like and it comes into play here as well. If we do not take care of our minds and bodies, anxiety can and will set in. This anxiety then turns into a variety of physical effects on the body.

Before we get into the short-term and long-term effects of anxiety, let's discuss a few of the anxiety diagnosis I have read about. First, there is social anxiety. This is when someone gets very anxious in crowds, large or small. There is a fear of being judged or humiliated in public. Second, there is post-traumatic stress disorder (PTSD). This occurs after a traumatic life event, whether you witnessed it or experienced it. It can be all the sudden or not show up for years. Third, there are panic attacks! This one we discussed in the previous chapter and comes on all the sudden! These are just a few of the anxiety diagnosis that I have read about or personally experienced. I am sure that there are many more that I do not know about and your best option is to discuss it with your medical doctor for a proper diagnosis and treatment plan.

Now that we have an idea of what the types of anxiety are, let's discuss the short-term effects of anxiety. These may vary by person and some people may only experience one or two of these. During an anxiety attack, as I stated in my story before, you may experience sudden shortness of breath or a racing heart. This can be very scary if you have never experienced an anxiety attack before. You feel as though your heart is beating through your chest. Another physical effect is constant exhaustion and trouble sleeping. You can fall asleep, but you cannot stay asleep. You wake up with your mind racing about all the things you must accomplish that day. This, in turn, causes you to feel constantly drained. Your body needs time to rest and rejuvenate at night. Some people with anxiety experience achy muscles, not necessarily during the attack but this we will go into further detail with the long-term effects of anxiety. Other physical effects include constant stomach aches, sweaty palms, easily startled and shaky, and tightness in your throat. One of the biggest physical effects of the body that I experienced during my time as a teacher was coming down with colds or the flu constantly. It seemed that every year I got a severe cold or even the flu. People would say, oh you work around kids, so your body needs to get immune to the viruses. Nope, that was not it at all. I suffered from anxiety. I didn't sleep at night. I didn't get the rest I needed. I was constantly drained. My mind was constantly in a state of panic about what I needed to get done. My doctor would tell me all the time, you need to rest. Your body and mind need to rest. And all of this tied to not resting, bad self-care, anxiety and eventually long-term physical sickness.

We have discussed the short-term effects of anxiety on the body and now I would like to talk more about the long-term physical effects. For me, the short-term and long-term effects went hand in hand and I really never understood why I always felt so bad, until now. One physical effect is unexplained muscle aches and pains. But remember when your body doesn't get the rest it needs, aches and pains will happen. Constant irritability and increased depression are other long-term effects of anxiety. When you become tired, you get irritable. People do not want to be around you because you are being mean and hateful. This is a domino effect and can cause you to spiral into a state of depression. Do you see how all of these effects can be tied together? For me, the one long-term physical effect was constant headaches. No matter what I did or where I went, I always had a headache. Some of the headaches were so debilitating that I needed to be in a dark room, no sound, and no one bothering me. I would use a heating pad on my back and a cold compress on my head. These headaches would take over my life! I even went to the emergency room once and was crying so bad the doctor gave me a shot that put me out. These physical effects are no joke and can take a toll on a person.

Other educators have indicated that they have experienced similar short-term and long-term physical effects due to anxiety and stress. Some to the point where they had to quit teaching in order to work on their health. Some are to this day contemplating other careers due to the stress of teaching. This goes back to my research on the factors of burnout and why we cannot keep teachers in the field. Other educators try and work through the physical effects and use the long periods of time off to recoup. When is enough, enough? Society wants to discuss mental health issues for students and criminals but where is the discussion on mental-health for educators? What are we doing to help our educators?

Chapter 4 – Understanding Anxiety – A Teacher's Perspective

Teacher's often feel like their feelings are not taken into consideration when anxious events happen in and out of the classroom. What people do not understand is that an anxious moment in the classroom can and often does carry over into the personal life of the educator. I wanted to dig deeper into the lives of teachers who are managing anxiety and get their perspective on how they cope and continue to teach while managing their anxiety. Below are different interviews that I conducted with teachers that are currently experiencing anxiety while teaching. Names have been changed to protect the privacy of each individual educator, but their stories will shock you and hopefully, society will start to understand why we need to assist our educators through these events instead of making them feel like they do not matter.

Teacher 1 Interview

Dr. Scott:

Welcome teacher one. Thank you for joining me today. Okay. The first question I have for you is, could you briefly describe what your anxiety symptoms are?

Teacher 1:

I don't sleep well. I have a hard time sleeping at night. I can't shut my brain off. I'm constantly going over things that are happening in the classroom and how to deal with it. I don't eat right. I tend to eat the wrong things and I binge eat. Because I get so hurt, you know, and it's like self-medicating cause I don't drink, don't smoke. I don't have time for friends cause I'm so busy with my job. I'll come home cause a lot of times I don't move during the day. I don't eat until two, three o'clock just because I'm so busy. I don't have time to stop because my classroom, my students are with me from 6:45 AM until they leave. You know, they're the only time they're away is part sometimes during their second period when they have an elective. But most of the time they come back early, or they leave late. So, they're just with me all day long. And I'm constantly doing this, this, this and this. So, by the time I'm done, I get off work. It's like ahhhhhh.

Teacher 1:

I come home and then I eat the wrong things. And that's probably one of my worst anxiety symptoms. Sometimes headaches. I get a lot of headaches. Those are some of the worst things I think that I suffer from.

Dr. Scott:

So, the physical symptoms you have are just lack of sleeping really bad headaches, not eating correctly.

Teacher 1:

Yeah. It's not eating correctly and, and they've given me so much now. Every year it's just gotten a little bit worse and a little bit worse to the point now that I can't, I don't even have time to go to the gym. I don't even have time to go for a walk because I just got home right before you called me. I just got home.

Dr. Scott:

So, no opportunities for self-care.

Teacher 1:

Hmm. Very, very little.

Dr. Scott:

Have you sought out any kind of professional help for anxiety or are you trying to deal with this on your own?

Teacher 1:

Just mainly trying to deal with it on my own. My son had a therapist for a while. He was going for a couple of years and sometimes, you know, he would have me come in and talk to me separately because I'm the primary caregiver for my son. So that was probably the closest thing I had to therapy.

Dr. Scott:

Okay. So, can you give me just an example or two of some situations that have given you the most anxiety?

Teacher 1:

Oh Wow. Well this year, they took and combined the VV classes with the CPI class. So, I've always had a CPI school. Now I've got these students are higher socially, so I've got EBD students in my classroom now and you know, they're in there with my pre k level students. And so, it's just keeping all of those, you know, managing all those behaviors and managing all those temperaments and managing all the stuff that's going on in the classroom is a huge amount of stress. Then they decided not only do I have my IEPs, but I now have seven consult kids that I am responsible for. So, the paperwork load has increased tremendously. They just hired a new teacher. They've had, there's, there have been two CDI teachers now for the last couple of years, but the last one was just quit. And they just hired a new one. She has no clue what she's doing. So, I'm having to do all of the other paperwork for what we do.

Dr. Scott:

How many total on your caseload right now?

Teacher 1:

On my caseload right now, it is 23 I have 18 students on my own and then the rest are consults.

Dr. Scott:

Oh wow, that is a lot. So, you really don't have any time for anything else?

Teacher 1:

No, because I work, I leave the house in the morning at 6:15 and I get to work by 6:45 AM. I work all day long because I'm constantly with students. I mentioned behaviors. I have kids with physical needs, so I have one, he has to be helped in the bathroom and the other females in the room don't feel comfortable. So, he's my responsibility. So, I'm in the bathroom with him. I'm dealing with parents; I'm dealing with a lot of stuff. And you can't do an IEP in that environment. I've got, three paraprofessionals in there. They did give me another paraprofessional, so I have three now. So, we've got three adults plus me plus 18 students. I got two students in these big electric wheelchairs. We are just crammed in this room and we're literally kind of on top of each other.

Dr. Scott:

I understand.

Teacher 1:

And then they've given me one student who really should be at a different school because he sits in the corner and screams a good part of the day, you know, and curses at the other students. And then that sets off my EBD students who get angry. So, I'm constantly managing all these behaviors, including the feelings and emotions of my parents' actions because sometimes they're tired, they're exasperated. So, I have to step in, and you know, deal with them too. So, it's like you're talking about 18 students and three adults that I'm managing all these behaviors and it's extremely stressful.

Dr. Scott:

Well, and I think that puts another layer on your anxiety too. We don't think about the paras that we manage in the classroom and we do manage them in the classroom just like we manage the students. But I wonder how much anxiety they have as well in the classroom. So how do you handle, when you start getting anxiety in your classroom, how do you handle that? What do you do?

Teacher 1:

Well, the thing I've learned to do that helps me the most is to just focus on one thing at a time. If I start thinking about the enormity of everything and everything that's going on, I start to feel so overwhelmed and my anxiety goes through the roof. So, what I do is I figure out this is the next thing I need to do. This is what I need to focus on. And I just keep my eyes on that, and I don't think about the rest of it if that makes any sense.

Dr. Scott:

No, it makes perfect sense. So how do you handle it when you get home? Do you see that your anxiety gets higher when you get home? Does it get lower when you get home? How do you handle things when you're at home?

Teacher 1:

As soon as the students leave in the afternoon, once we get them out of there and get them on the buses and get them home, you know, I feel like my anxiety level comes down quite a bit because I've had several incidents in the classroom. I've been attacked several times. You know, and I've had some very violent students. I had one that for a year was just with me all the time. So, I would be in a room alone with him. And three different times he attacked me, and I mean he was a big student because these are, these are high school students. He was a very large student and the last time they came in he was trying to break my arm and he was about to bite my face and they took three of them to pull him off me. I think I still have some residuals from that. So, there's always that sort of anxiety level of is somebody going to go off? Cause I have five students with behavioral plans, right. I have an EBD student and I have one student that is extremely low, and he is a huge behavior issue. He doesn't listen, he won't sit down, he curses at the other students, spits at people, you know, so he sets off all the other students and so soon as they leave my anxiety level automatically, just that constant fear is something going to happen with someone sort of drops.

Dr. Scott:

So, it gets lower when you're at home versus being in the classroom?

Teacher 1:

Yeah. It's a different kind of anxiety when I come home, it's the anxiety of, okay, my mom needs me to do this. Do I have time to get this done? She needs help with this. My son needs help with that, my daughter. But it's not that sort of, okay, is somebody going to lose it and start attacking somebody type of fear.

Dr. Scott:

Have you ever felt that your anxiety from school has spilled over into your home life?

Teacher 1:

Oh yeah. A lot. It has a huge effect on my home. What I'm really working this year is making sure I'm not bringing this stuff home. Cause I would come home and I've had a horrible day, you know, I've been hollered at by administration or by parents I'd bring that home and then I'm barking at my own family and it's like I'm learning to just not bring this home. I try hard not to bring that home.

And if I've had a bad day, I'll tell my daughter, you know, hey, I've had a really bad day. My stress levels are through the roof. Just let me have a little time to kind of let go.

Dr. Scott:

Right. Good. At least you're starting to do that. Self-care is so important to what we do. So, the last question that I have is what would you really want to say to people so that they know and understand what teachers are going through during their periods of anxiety?

Teacher 1:

I don't think they realize the level of anxiety. I think people assume that this is an easy job. You're sitting down all day, you know, you're just teaching kids, you are inside. It's a nice environment, but they don't realize that you have all these responsibilities with paperwork and much more. You know, everybody's always worried about getting sued. The district's worried about getting sued. Teachers are worried about getting sued. So, there's all these checks and things you've got to look out for. So, you're always worried about that. You're always trying to manage this and that, and meetings that you're responsible for and all this other stuff. And it's just like we felt like you're going in a hundred different directions and I don't think people that have not been in the field understand that. And the people that make decisions, you know, the ones that tell us you need to do this and this and this, with this paperwork, have no clue what we do.

Teacher 1:

So, it sounds good on paper. It sounds right on paper, but there's no possible way for you to do it. It's impossible. They want us to do, especially for Special Ed, you know, and it's absolutely impossible. I mean, I have 18 students at all these different levels, all these different IEP levels that I'm supposed to be monitoring their accommodations and I'm supposed to be monitoring their IEP goals and supposed to be progress monitoring them. And I'm supposed to be managing behaviors and I'm supposed to be doing 15 million other things at the same time. I have to go off campus all day and Friday with them. And then they have CBI's that I have to complete the paperwork for that, and now there's a dress code that they have implemented. These students are not rich, but they want them to dress nicely to go on the job site. So, I'm like, how am I supposed to do that? So now I'm responsible for locating some dressy clothes and then getting them to change them before they go on the job site.

Dr. Scott:

Do you teach all academics plus vocational?

Teacher 1:

Yeah, I do. I think the last time I counted; 19 courses are coded to my name. So, I teach four English. I teach four math, I teach three science, I teach three histories, I teach two career classes. And then I have them from ninth grade to postsecondary. Some of them stay until age 22. And there is no curriculum. The district I teach in and we don't have curriculum, we don't have any. So, what do I do, what do I use? I have to create stuff that is for them on each level.

Dr. Scott:

So that puts another level on top of everything else that you have to do. The teaching, the paperwork, the IEP meeting and now creating curriculum. Those are huge factors of burnout. When I did my research on secondary special ed teacher burnout, hose were the huge issues that my participants indicated were the reasons they were leaving teaching.

Teacher 1:

Yeah, I've considered it. I really have talked very seriously about it. The new teacher that just came in and came from another state and her first question to me was where the curriculum is. I said we don't have much here, what assessments do we get? I said, whatever, you can figure out, whatever you can find online for free or you can buy. I think because we don't have meetings. There really isn't anything that we have. Figure it out on your own. So, when I first came into this classroom, they hadn't had a teacher for a while. She got fired and so there were substitutes and all they had were some old regular textbooks from the general education classes. And so, I was using those for a while. I realize this is totally way above what they can do. They're not understanding any of this. And the previous teacher had the higher ones sitting there copying notes out of the books.

Teacher 1:

And the other ones, the lower functioning kids were sitting there doodling and that was what she had been doing. And then she would teach a little bit out of these textbooks. I'm like, okay, this is never going to work for these students. And so, I slowly started changing things. I have three groups now that are broken out by levels. So, I have to go find things that relate to that.

Dr. Scott:

So, do you have anybody that you can go to on your campus to explain to them how anxious you are, or your anxiety levels are high up that?

Teacher 1:

No. No, we hardly see our boss anymore. She's all, I'm busy, I'm busy, I'm busy, I'm busy. So, we don't really see her anymore. And I think her whole point now is to keep her head down and get out. She doesn't really want to hear any problems. And if I try to bring up anything, well we're all busy. You know, I'm really busy too. And it's like, well I get that. But you know.

Dr. Scott:

So, for your personal care, for your own wellbeing, do you have an employee assistance program?

Teacher 1:

Not that I know of, no. We don't really have any. When I took this job, I got a set of keys and that was it. And then I get two boxes of paper a year and one ink cartridge, which doesn't even begin to cover what I have to do. So, No. Everything that I buy myself, I go buy the paper, I go by the rubber gloves because I have to change kids in the bathroom, you know, I have to deal with a lot of stuff. Sometimes they'll give me some, but a lot of times there won't, there's nothing in the budget so I just go and get it myself.

Dr. Scott:

Do you have a special education coordinator at the district level?

Teacher 1:

We do and she kind of tries. The district I've worked for has what's called principal autonomy, which means that each principal decides how things are done and our principal is an okay guy. But I think his philosophy is, you know, I don't want to know. I've never been to a CPI classroom. I don't understand how they work. Just do what you need to do and keep it quiet as much as possible.

Dr. Scott:

Yeah. And I think that puts another level again on us as teachers when we don't have that administrator support, which spikes our anxiety again and is really bad for our mental health that we do not have that support that we need. So, society needs to know that mental health for teachers is very important. That we need support from our administrators. We need support from our community, from our parents. And our anxiety levels are very high, very high.

Teacher 1:

I was just going to say I used to be a 911 operator for a university campus police. I worked in a law firm as a paralegal. You know, I held different jobs, and this is honestly is the most stressful job of any I've had.

Dr. Scott:

Yeah, I agree. When I first got into teaching, I didn't think it was going to be that stressful. I used to hear all the time, oh, you're off for the summers. You know, you have it so easy. You're a teacher, you're off for the summer, but you have no clue what I went through in the classroom for those months that I was in there. So, I hear what you're going through and it's the exact same thing that I went through.

Teacher 1:

You see the thing is I don't have summers off because I teach ESY, so I'm working all summer. That's the money I put aside to purchase the boxes of paper and the rubber gloves, the ink cartridges, and stuff that I need to run my class so that my students don't go without. You know, if I don't have work to give them, then I'm going to have behavior issues, a lot more behaviors. So, I'll work ESY this summer in order to afford to be able to pay for everything I need. And then as far as time off, I, you know, I very rarely, when I have a day off, I'm working. I'm sitting here working on Saturday. I either work all day Saturday or all-day Sunday doing lesson plans. Doing my flip charts, figuring out what my curriculum is for that week, getting an IEP done. It's constant work with no time off.

Dr. Scott:

Yeah, no, I completely understand. Okay. Thank you. Thank you so much for helping me with this. I appreciate your time in telling your story!

Teacher 2 Interview

Dr. Scott:

Hello! I want to welcome teacher two. So, the first question that I have for you is, can you describe your anxiety symptoms when you're having them?

Teacher 2:

Do you want to know my anxiety symptoms at work or before work or when I come home?

Dr. Scott:

Let's talk about at work first and then later there are questions about what you do at home.

Teacher 2:

My anxiety symptoms are mostly like my chest. Like it feels really tight. You know, you have that kind of sensation where you feel like you can't breathe. You obviously know that you can. And then sometimes irritability and just, it's hard to focus sometimes cause there's so much going on and there's so much that needs to be done. Sometimes I think it's overwhelming to try to prioritize all the things that need to be done.

Dr. Scott:

Okay. So, can you give me an example of a specific situation where you've had the most anxiety?

Teacher 2:

It's usually one. Since I do teach adapted behavior and specifically this year, I have a lot of students that can get physical. Knowing what staff, I can put in. What places and I'm always anticipating what if this happens? What if that happens? But I don't have enough. I have more needs than I have people. So, I just have to kind of trust that it's just going to go okay. And I like, I have my radio on all the time. Like, you know, they're going to call me, they're going to call me. So, I feel like I can't even be 100% into what I'm doing. Does that make sense?

Dr. Scott:

Yes, it does make sense. So, when you're at work and you're starting to feel anxious, how do you handle it? What do you do?

Teacher 2:

Okay, go on. You have to keep moving forward.

Dr. Scott:

Okay. So, do you have any coping strategies that you use when you are at work?

Teacher 2:

I just have to be very self-reflective. I do have an anxiety medication I can take as needed, but that's not my go-to. I just have to be reflective and be all, you know, think of what I can do to change what's going on now. And then I just have to kind of sit back and prioritize what I need to do and what I can do for myself and what I can do for my students. Like is me getting upset, going to help the situation. Is me reacting going to help? You know, what am I doing to make things better or worse.

Dr. Scott:

Right. So, when did you first notice your anxiety levels were higher?

Teacher 2:

That would've been a couple of years ago when I was crying in my classroom closet.

Dr. Scott:

Okay. How many years ago was that?

Teacher 2:

I'm going to say five years ago.

Dr. Scott:

And that's when you first started teaching?

Teacher 2:

No, that was like a year and a half into teaching.

Dr. Scott:

Okay. So how does your anxiety compare at home versus at work?

Teacher 2:

I think I have more anxiety at home.

Dr. Scott:

Why do you have more at home?

Teacher 2:

Because of my students specifically, I am worried about what happens to them when they go home. So, I'm constantly thinking about that. And I am just anticipating what is going to happen the next day.

Dr. Scott:

And then, so what do you do at home that helps you not be so anxious?

Teacher 2:

I drink wine. I usually call my mom. You know, I talk about it, I'll exercise, I will watch TV. Just kind of do some me-time stuff.

Dr. Scott:

That's good that you're doing self-care though. A lot of people that I talked to indicated that they don't even have time for any kind of self-care, which makes it extremely stressful for them. So, you're way ahead.

Teacher 2:

Oh good. I'm doing something right.

Dr. Scott:

Yes, you are. So, my last question is what do you want people to know and understand about teachers with anxiety?

Teacher 2:

What do you I want people to know and understand?

Dr. Scott:

Just society in general, I don't think society understands the difficulties in teaching. And if you had an opportunity to tell society, what would you want to tell them about why teachers have anxiety?

Teacher 2:

I think that we as educators have anxiety because I think that society is also expecting us as the school staff to raise, counsel, educate, discipline, etc. they're children. I think that we have a lot more pressure on us to do more than just teach to, you know, do data and all these things. Other things that we're also doing all the other things.

Dr. Scott:

So that we're, we're doing parent job and teacher job all in one seven to eight hour a day.

Teacher 2:

Yes. I think what we don't give ourselves enough grace. It's okay for our kids to have a bad day and it's okay for our kids to have anxiety and for our kids to struggle with mental health or personal self-care things. But we don't allow ourselves to have that kind of day. We don't allow ourselves to deal with anxiety. I think that we just feel like we just have to keep going.

Dr. Scott:

Yeah. And I agree. I think that part of the issue is, it's a taboo subject. Nobody wants to talk about mental health care for educators. Nobody wants to do anything about it because educators are held at such a higher standard. I mean, they get in trouble for the smallest post on Facebook or social media. And I think that puts a lot of anxiety on people too.

Teacher 2:

Well, yeah, I mean, and you can't, I just feel like even when it comes to, when you talk about the things that you're struggling with, one, it makes you probably feel inadequate because I know it does for me, and that makes you feel that you are not doing your job to the best of your ability. And I think it makes you feel like, you know, you kind of suck at what you're doing. Sometimes you need help and a lot of people don't want to admit it.

Dr. Scott:

Well, and I think it goes back to administrative support to, our administrators need to know that we're only human and that we need extra support during these very stressful times and we don't need to be made to feel inadequate and insecure and like we're bad teachers or even bad human beings because we are having a bad day.

Teacher 2:

I totally agree. And like I was wondering if I should even say this, but you know, I'm kind of at the end of my rope. Like I had previously shared, you know, I am looking for a new job. I cannot continue to put myself in the same situation every day. And I was at one point last week where

I was like do, I just need to walk down to my principal's office and be like, look, this is not working for me. I'm sorry. Is there another place that you can put me in the building, but I didn't because how was that going to make me look?

Dr. Scott:

Right. I've had other teachers say that they feel like when they go in for support, it makes them feel like they look weak and insecure.

Teacher 2:

I agree. Well and then you know, cause then there's always chatter, and you know, we all are aware of it, but you know, like, oh whoa, well she can't handle this, or she can't handle all that, you know.

Dr. Scott:

And I had one teacher tell me that we need to have an environment that makes us feel safe and supported. That we don't need the fear of being seen as too emotional, weak or unprofessional. And when we have those panic attacks or anxiety in the classroom, that she felt like she was being judged for having a bad day and when she went to her administrator for support.

Teacher 2:

I agree and I've had the same experience. I've been told this year by one specific administrator you know, well, when so-and-so sees us, we must be composed, we have to do this. We have to be on the same page. Well, we're not on the same page because you were breaking the law and we're not on the same page because you are not working with these students every day and you are coming into the back end.

Dr. Scott:

So, they're not visible, not visible administrators, which goes back to my first book when I talked about factors of burnout. When I did all that research, that was a lot of the factors of burnout and why teachers were leaving. It's just, it seems like it all comes back to that.

Teacher 2:

Well, I think administrators at my current job are more visible than at my previous school. But still like, and I don't know if maybe they think specifically like Special Ed, you know, they're not calling us like we want to stay out of their hair or what. So, it's either like they're too involved where they're like, oh, I'll take over, I'll take over. Or they're just not involved at all. It's, it's one extreme to the other.

Dr. Scott:

I completely understand. Well, those are all my questions. So, I want to thank you for helping me with my research.

Teacher 2:

Thank you for having me.

Teacher 3 Interview

Dr. Scott:

Hello and thank you so much for being here today. I truly appreciate it. We're going to just start by talking about your anxiety symptoms. If you could briefly describe your anxiety symptoms inside the classroom.

Teacher 3:

Oh Gosh. Okay. I would say the biggest one would be probably like my mind racing. And then there's kind of like a flight or fight response. You know, where your heart is racing and you kind of feel like you want to bolt but you know, you can't.

Dr. Scott:

Right. So, your fight or flight kicks in and then you can't shut your mind off. It's racing all of the time. Is that consistent every day for you right now?

Teacher 3:

No, not right now.

Dr. Scott:

Okay. Tell me about a specific incident that triggered your anxiety

Teacher 3:

I would say one that's for sure. I had an administrator at my first job that wrote an evaluation that was based on false information. So, that was a pretty big anxiety trigger for me.

Teacher 3:

In the classroom, the biggest times were probably when students were highly escalated to the point where they were like physically aggressive.

Dr. Scott:

Were you ever hurt in the classroom?

Teacher 3:

Yes.

Dr. Scott:

Did you ever seek out professional help for your anxiety after you were hurt in the classroom?

Teacher 3:

Yeah.

Dr. Scott:

Okay. And did that help?

Teacher 3:

Yeah. I actually still see a counselor every couple of months or so. Just to keep things in check.

Dr. Scott:

Okay, that is great that you continue to see a counselor. How do you handle your anxiety when you feel it coming on? You know you're going to have this anxiety attack. How do you deal with it while you're in the classroom?

Teacher 3:

Actually, kind of depends on the situation. Anytime I can, there's a couple of coworkers that I have gotten to know really well and trust. Anytime that I can process with them, they really helped but that is not always an option right away. I guess it kind of varies situation by situation a lot of times. I have to remind myself that I have everything planned out and I know where things are headed, things like that.

Dr. Scott:

So more like a self-reflection, self-check during the day. So, do you see any of this anxiety transferring to your home life when you come home from work?

Teacher 3:

Oh yeah.

Dr. Scott:

And how do you deal with it at home?

Teacher 3:

The best way I found to deal with it is just kind of drawing a line because it's really easy to get caught up in all the paperwork and lesson planning, and you know all those other acronyms that we have to manage. I found the best thing I can do is set a time for myself where I cut that off and I say, now my school is over. This is my time. And not letting the two merge together too much.

Dr. Scott:

Right. Okay. Well, this is kind of your opportunity to tell people who don't understand or don't know about what it's like to teach with anxiety. What do you want them to know? If you could just tell anybody anything, what would you say about it?

Teacher 3:

For other teachers or people in general?

Dr. Scott:

I would say people in general because I feel like a lot of people don't understand that anxiety in teaching happens and they don't realize because a lot of people have a different perception of what teaching is. Everybody says, oh you get summers off so you can't have it that bad. I really feel like people don't have a good grasp on what teaching special education really is or even general education. So, if you could tell those people, what would you want them to know?

Teacher 3:

Well, I think a lot of people, as you said, don't understand the job expectations of a teacher. And especially for me being a special education teacher, I've had comments even from family members, like they don't seem to understand that I have all the responsibilities of the general education teacher. And then some when you pack on the IEP and evaluations and all of that. They almost seem to think that I just go to school and hang out with kids all day. And that's, you know, that's certainly part of my job. But it is not by any stretch of the imagination all that I do. Um, just the understanding that there is a lot of pressure and there are very high demands and a lot of times there are many high demands being placed on a teacher at once and they have to really learn to juggle those expectations. And learn to manage and prioritize. The prioritizing in itself can be really stressful for some people, I think.

Dr. Scott:

Right. No, I agree with you especially about the higher expectations of educators in general.

Teacher 3:

I think there's like you said, I think there's just a lot more expected of us than people that are not in the field realize.

Dr. Scott:

No, that's really good information. Those are all the questions that I have. So, I really want to thank you again for being here and helping me with all of this information.

Teacher 4 Interview

Dr. Scott:

I want to welcome teacher four today. We're going to go ahead and get started. Can you briefly describe your anxiety symptoms in the classroom?

Teacher 4:

It varies from year to year depending on my caseload. But the worst it's been is just headaches, a lot of headaches sweating, like a red rash and I'm just missing a lot of work, nausea and things like that.

Dr. Scott:

Have you sought out any professional help for your anxiety?

Teacher 4:

My first year I did, I went to counseling and then I'm on anti-anxiety medicine.

Dr. Scott:

Okay. And then can you describe a situation where you had the most anxiety?

Teacher 4:

Last year when I was like getting beat up almost daily by a student there was a lot of anxiety, especially when I was driving to work. I had about a 25-minute drive to work and I would always have to call a friend or something to keep me from getting anxious just because I didn't know what was going to come across, what was going to happen that day. Cause this student was injuring me to the fact that I had to go to the doctor a couple of times just to get x-rays. So, I didn't know what would occur that day.

Dr. Scott:

Okay. Did you take any time off?

Teacher 4:

Not from injuries but I took a lot of mental health days last year.

Dr. Scott:

When you feel anxious in the classroom? How do you handle it?

Teacher 4:

Well, I've tried to think that if my students are acting up to a point that I'm starting to feel anxious that they must be feeling anxious as well in some sort of way. So, I usually try to put on the meditation for myself or for them or I'll put on calming music. I usually have more than one adult in the room, so I'll try to take a walk. But then just try to distract myself. So, like maybe this one student who I know is always willing to work hard and be helpful. I will just sit with them and read with them to distract me because I know they won't give me a hard time or whatever.

Dr. Scott:

Those are some good coping strategies that you have there. Do you see that your anxiety transfers over from work to home?

Teacher 4:

Well, this year I wouldn't say it's as bad just because of the group I have this year, I have a very good rapport with them because this is my third year with a lot of them. But I don't have too much at home. It's like I have a lot when I'm driving, but I think that was honestly ignited by the situations I was going through last year and the anxiety when driving to work and it just transferred over to me driving in general.

Dr. Scott:

Okay. And then the last question that I have is if you could tell the world about teaching with anxiety and you wanted people to understand what that means, what would you tell them?

Teacher 4:

I think more people battle it than we realize, and I don't think we're all alone. And the best thing that we can do is kind of just to help each other and a simple smile or how are you doing? That can really go a long way.

Dr. Scott:

That's awesome. Thank you so much for sharing with us today.

As you can see from teacher one's interview the caseload size, the lack of support from administration, and the behaviors in the classroom contribute to the teacher's level of anxiety. There is no time for self-care because of the responsibilities placed on this teacher. What you cannot get from the printed interview is the tone of voice from this teacher, the despair in the voice of the teacher, and the exhaustion I could see while speaking to teacher 1. Each interview had a different perspective on the level of anxiety that is experienced in the classroom from being "beaten-up" daily as one teacher described to the loads of additional paperwork or responsibilities that another teacher described. Anxiety is taking a toll on the mental health of our teachers, what are we doing about it?

Chapter 5 – Trauma in the Classroom

We have discussed a lot about anxiety including some perspectives from educators. Another important factor that triggers anxiety and what really needs to be discussed is trauma in the classroom. Not trauma from a student perspective but when a teacher gets hurt in the classroom.

We've all heard of PTSD and what that means but let me put it into another perspective for you. When a teacher gets injured in the classroom by a student there is a certain amount of PTSD that happens afterward. Now it may not happen immediately but eventually, it catches up to that teacher and causes a downward spiral into anxiety, depression, and PTSD.

Let me start by saying I personally have experienced being injured in the classroom by a student. Now it wasn't a simple injury where I could work afterward. It was a full-blown injury where I had ribs out of place and I had to take some time off of work. I haven't spoken about this injury since it happened nor have, I discussed with anyone the aftereffects of what has been going on with me for fear of being judged in all categories that come with being an educator. Now I believe is the time, for more of a therapy's sake than anything, to discuss this.

I was in my third year as a special education teacher and our year started off very stressful without being fully staffed. My teaching partner and I were the only ones there to help the subs navigate this unknown world of special education they had been thrown into. We had some really great subs and then we had some subs that were well, not so great. Throughout the year we had to deal with many things and the stress of the profession was getting to all of us! I had over fifteen kids in my classroom with five other adults and all those students need some type of one-to-one attention. We had feedings, rest rooming, and we had those with behavior issues.

The day I got injured there were a lot of behavior issues we were all dealing with. We had on some calming music and had the lights low for sensory issues. I was dealing with one of the behavior issues when the student kicked me in my upper chest, and I fell back onto the floor. It knocked the breath out of me, and I was dazed. A para and a sub came to my rescue, while the other paras in the classroom dealt with the other students. Now, keep in mind, I was the only teacher of record for this classroom, working with a really great sub and three paraprofessionals. I got up off the floor and went crying out of the room, sat in the hallway, and drank some water. I made it through most of the afternoon, but the sub talked me into going to urgent care and I am really glad I did. I got x-rays and the doctor indicated that I, in fact, had a rib out of place, it wasn't broken but it was very painful. I took the next day off but after trying to return back to work on several occasions, I just couldn't do it. I was in pain. I couldn't lift my arm. I couldn't lift a cup of coffee it hurt so bad. It was time for me to take a leave of absence.

I cried for days. Not because I was hurt and let me tell you it hurt like hell! No, I cried because I felt like a failure. I felt like I let down my parents, my kids, my campus, and the staff that I worked with. I was a great teacher! I had a lot of experience in dealing with students with behaviors. But I was not prepared for the toll it would take on me mentally by getting injured in the classroom and that is what I want to tell everyone in this chapter.

The pain you feel from a physical injury is nothing to sneeze at but the mental anguish during and after is another thing. I was mentally, physically, and emotionally exhausted on a daily basis. I couldn't sleep, I barely ate, I had a constant stomachache, I was irritable and would snap at my husband. And honestly, people would say that I looked like hell. I was hurt and I didn't know how this could possibly happen to me. Someone that was so careful and that always put the needs of the students first. How could I be so distracted that a student could get that close to kicking the crap out of me? These are the thoughts that would go streaming through my mind in the middle of the night. Other thoughts would be who is taking care of my kids, who is doing the paperwork, what about state testing?? I tried to find a therapist through our employee assistance program and could never find one that was accepting new patients. I tried online therapy, but I couldn't afford to continue with that as a self-pay and at the time it was not part of the employee assistance program. What was I going to do? Just curl up on the couch and cry myself to sleep every night? For me, this is when I turned to God for help. I downloaded a bible app and I started reading daily devotionals. I joined a couple of Christian social media groups that would help me. This helped me through the period of time I was out on leave and I thought that I was mentally ready to get back to work.

    I was out of work I think a good month and a half, and I went through physical therapy. I finally got my shoulder back to where I could get the doctor to release me to go back to work. I was excited to get back but not prepared mentally for what was about to happen. I was scared. I was scared to be back in my own classroom. I was scared of the student that kicked me. I was scared to be alone. I felt inadequate. I would have complete anxiety and panic attacks on the way to work and would speed to get home to my husband, dog, and couch. I felt like a horrible teacher and person for having all this anxiety. I literally bathed in lavender and peppermint oil to help with the anxiety. I am sure that both my staff and my students didn't appreciate that smell all day, every day! I would try and keep busy in the classroom to mask the anxiety of everything that was going on in my mind and I am not sure if that even worked. When I would finally get home, I would immediately get into my pajamas and curl up on the couch.

Again, I wouldn't sleep at night because of the nightmares of what happened and now I was back in the classroom. I didn't go out with my friends anymore and I barely left the house. I couldn't explain to anyone what I was feeling. I didn't want to be judged. I didn't want people to think I was weak, and I didn't want the people that I worked with to know. I especially didn't want the parents to know what I was going through because I was there with their kids and I am supposed to be the strong one in the classroom. At least that was my thought process. That was a big mistake on my part because to this day I am still dealing with tons of anxiety that I feel stims from this exact incident. Now, I do not think it was the only thing causing my anxiety. I was also going through the doctoral journey at the same time which puts a different amount of stress and anxiety on you. But I do feel that it is the whole teaching experience that threw me, my body, and my mind into a state of panic. We've discussed before the tremendous amount of stress and pressure a special education teacher is under. It is compounded by severe behaviors in the classroom and even more when a teacher gets injured.

  I left that campus and the district simply because I couldn't handle the anxiety of being back in that classroom, I needed a fresh start somewhere else, and I was presented with a wonderful opportunity in a new district. I spent the next year in a smaller classroom with different students. I had a great year with only one major panic attack when a student raised a chair to throw it at me. But my administrator helped me work through it and that was huge for me! I had a great year and ended my public teaching career on a positive note.

We've since moved to a new city where I thought that I could at least sub in the district that I am living in and this is when the anxiety has hit me again. I've barely left the house. I don't want to go anywhere or do anything. I simply just want to rest. Why is that, I keep thinking to myself? What is going on? I had a great last year in the classroom and my anxiety was finally starting to level out. So, what brought on this anxiety again. It is the thought of being in an unknown classroom again and getting hurt. All the trauma, anxiety, and PTSD from before has reared its ugly head again. I am signed up to sub, but I have not been able to accept any positions yet because I go into a state of panic every time I see that number ringing my phone. That is when I decided to research anxiety, mental health, and trauma in the classroom. It is an issue. It needs to be discussed. Teachers need mental health days. They need professional development training on issues just as this, anxiety, trauma in the classroom, self-care, and basically how to take care of ourselves when incidents like this happen. Districts are all about mental health for students but what about the mental health of your educators?? What is your district doing? My old district had an employee assistance program that didn't do me any good. What is your district doing about EAP's when they fail their educators? What is in place for those of us that do get injured in the classroom and have residual effects of the trauma?

I've heard so many other stories from teachers who have been injured in the classroom. Some have decided that medication is the best way to handle stress. Others have decided enough is enough and they are getting out. One educator told me that some of the comments to her and others have been that they knew what this job was all about and they took it anyway. And while I completely understand that in special education, there is some chance that you will get hurt, it should not be used as an excuse as to why teachers are getting injured. We are teachers just like anyone else and we want to educate, on whatever level that may be. We don't want to be constantly beaten up in the classroom and be told: "oh well it is your job and you accepted it". NO! That is not okay to say to anyone that is constantly being attacked in the classroom. We need help! We are begging for help in our own way! We are reaching out, so help us! Get us some mental health days! Get us some extra help in the classroom especially when we are dealing with extreme behavior kids. HELP US, we are crying out for it!

Today, I am in a much better place and have moved on from all the anxiety of the past. Writing this book and learning more about anxiety has helped me to become a better person, a better educator, a better leader, and a better wife. But it takes time to work through the anxious feeling and all the other thoughts that come with that. The thought of being less, the thought of being judged by everyone, that thought that you are not doing a good job, and the horrific thought that someone will find out and completely criticize you for your feelings is on the mind of every teacher who experiences anxiety, PTSD, or panic attacks.

Teachers are afraid to speak out in fear of being judged or even worse losing their jobs. Our teachers need support, they need help, and they need to not be judged when situations such as this happen. We need professional development on self-care, on burnout, on anxiety, and on how to take care of us so we can ultimately take care of our students. What will you do to help a teacher?

Chapter 6 – Self-Care During Periods of Anxiety

In my first book, I wrote a chapter on self-care techniques where I interviewed Emily, a health care coach. She discussed some very important techniques that I want to get into deeper details about in this chapter. Hopefully, some of these techniques you as an educator can implement into your own life to assist in decreasing your anxiety. Some of these self-care techniques tie in with the next chapter of coping with anxiety! Self-care is very important especially during times of anxiety. Remember if you do not take care of your mind and body it is not healthy for you.

One of the self-care techniques my doctor use to stress all the time was exercise. You have to make time to exercise your body. She indicated that physical exercise can help decrease anxiety. Now, I know this can be difficult depending on you. For me, it makes me more anxious to get out and walk or run somewhere. I have to talk myself into it every time. But once I get out and I make it back, I feel better. There are many ways to get physical exercise. You can swim, you can walk on a treadmill, take a walk with a spouse, or go for a run. My doctor recommended twenty minutes of exercise a day. I do have to be honest with you though and tell you that I am not the best at keeping up with the physical exercise part. Before you begin an exercise routine please check with your primary care doctor. They may have other suggestions for you based on your needs and health.

Another technique suggested by my doctor was meditation or yoga. Now, this is something that I can do in my home! I have a room set-up that I can use for meditation. This is a technique that I use at night prior to going to bed. I turn out the lights, light some candles, and put on some calming music. You can even use an app that guides you through meditation. If you can, sign up for a yoga class and make yourself go at least once every two weeks. You can work up to every week if you want. You may even start slow and make a plan to go once a month. If you cannot go out, do it at home, it is worth the time!

Now, this next technique is hard for a lot of people, me included. Lower the caffeine intake. Yep, I said it, don't drink as much caffeine as you currently do. If you drink five cups of coffee a day, lower it to three. If you drink six sodas a day, lower it to three. This one was hard at first because of the physical symptoms I experienced while doing this were tough. I got really bad headaches but once I lowered it, it was much easier on me. My doctor indicated that caffeine increases your fight or flight behaviors and can increase your anxiety. Again, before you make any drastic changes in your routines, consult your doctor. I am not advocating that you completely cut out all caffeine suddenly but lowering it slowly will help with your anxiety.

Another self-care technique is to get some good rest. My doctor told me all the time that I needed a good sleep habit. Well, what does that mean? She told me that I need to go to sleep at the same time every night, no matter what! But before I went to bed, I needed to let my brain rest. I know that sounds weird but if I went straight from working on IEP's to bed, I found my mind was still racing as to what I had to get finished. I didn't get good sleep at that point and became very anxious. So, you need time to wind down even before bed. Again, this goes back to meditation, taking a walk, or even just sitting outside looking at the stars. Make sure you drink water before bed and not a soda or anything with caffeine in it. And reduce your alcohol and tobacco intake before bed. Also, the one thing I still have a hard time with is reducing noise in the bedroom. I like to fall asleep with the TV on, but my doctor has said this does not allow you to fall into a deep sleep and doesn't give you the rest you need. I still struggle with this one!

Next, find a support system. Whether it be a friend or an online community that you can talk to about your anxiety or what is happening. I know these days that the internet can be harmful, but it can also be a useful tool! For me, I found an online bible community where I could share daily devotionals as well as receive them. This is what helped me get through a really tough situation in a previous classroom when I could not find the support, I needed through an employee assistance program. To this day I am still receiving and sending out daily devotionals!

Finally, if none of these self-care techniques have worked for you, it is time to seek professional help. Just because you do seek this help does not make you a bad teacher or person. Let's be clear on that because I know from personal experience how bad you can feel when there is nowhere or no one to turn to for help. Get the help you need and take care of yourself. You cannot be the best you can be if you do not take care of yourself!

Chapter 7 – How to Cope with Anxiety

We have discussed a lot about anxiety in this book and touched on a few techniques. But how do you cope with anxiety? What are you really doing to manage it? You shouldn't just accept the fact that you have anxiety and push it aside and not deal with it. Anxiety is tough. It can run your life sometimes and you need to deal with the fact that you have it. There is nothing wrong with you. You are not less of a person because you have it. We constantly tell our students to use their coping strategies during periods of anxiety and as teachers, we need to do the same. Practice what you preach! Let's discuss some coping strategies that you can implement for yourself when you start to become anxious!

One of the techniques that I use is called grounding. There are several ways you can ground yourself during this time. But I use the 5-step method. You can do a 3-step method if you have less time. The 5-step method includes look, feel, listen, taste, and smell. Here is how it works for me!

1) Look around for 5 things you can see. Focus on them and name them as you are looking at them.

2) Feel four things and say them out loud. I can feel my shirt or my shoes. Or if you have a fidget, go for that! Whatever you can feel, use it.
3) Listen for three sounds that are around. What do hear? Do you hear students in the hall? Do you hear music? Name the three things you can hear out loud.
4) Smell two things. This is where my essential oils come in handy. I use peppermint and lavender oil daily. These are my two go-to things to smell. Lavender oil is a natural calming agent. If you have sensitive skin, you may consult your doctor before using it. There are several ways you can use both essential oils to smell. You can put it in a diffuser, directly on your skin, or on a cotton ball. If you do put it on your skin some of the best areas are your temples, bottom of your feet, wrists, or the back of your neck. Find something you can smell.
5) Taste one thing. Whether it is water or coffee or something to munch on. Grab something. Water normally is what I grab. Something about it is just soothing.

You can decrease these if you need and just implement a 3, 2, 1 program and pick the ones you want to do. Another technique I use is deep breathing. Take a few deep breaths in and exhale. We teach this technique all the time but how many of us actually use it ourselves? Remember start practicing what you are preaching.

I've heard and read about other techniques such as keeping yourself busy with housework or cleaning up an area. For me, that just makes my anxiety higher and has not worked. But for you, it may work out great. Another technique is to take a walk. If you are teaching this may not be a viable option at the moment. But if you can take a walk to the copy machine, the soda machine or to the front office. Get your mind off whatever is causing the anxiety. Remember that some anxiety is situational, and it helps to remove yourself from the situation if you can. A technique that we teach our students is counting. Count backward from ten while deep breathing. We have so many techniques that we use with our students in the classroom that would also be beneficial for us as educators to use. Start trying them out!

One of my favorite coping strategies to use is my dog. She is a registered emotional support animal (ESA) and she helps me during my periods of anxiety. She is loving and supportive which helps with my mental state. When I focus on her, I find that my stress levels and my anxiety decreased. I also find it interesting that she can sense when I am feeling anxious and she has an instinct of when she can help. She will come snuggle in my lap or start licking on me. She just knows! It is amazing how animals can help us. I do realize that not everyone can own a dog or cat for whatever reason but there are ways you can get your four-legged time in. You can volunteer at a shelter and provide love and snuggles to lonely pets. Do you have an elderly neighbor that has a pet, where you can volunteer to walk them, bathe them or just spend time with them? She is a constant in my world where everything is just spinning, and she has always been there for me to reduce my anxious feelings. There are multiple ways that you can find time with a furry friend and it is worth it. Find something that works for you and stick with it!

With all the talk about mental health for students, I felt it necessary to discuss the mental health of educators. It is so important that we take care of our teachers as well, but no one wants to talk about it. It's like some sort of taboo topic! Educators are often held to a higher standard, which makes it a difficult topic. No one wants to think of teachers as being human and making mistakes, but they do. Our teachers need to be made to feel loved even though they do make mistakes. One teacher told me she doesn't discuss her anxiety or her troubles in the classroom with anyone because she was belittled when she did. Is this the way we uplift the teachers that are with our children every day? Having anxiety doesn't make you a bad person. It doesn't make you less of a teacher and our teachers should be treated better!

Resources

I wanted a book that really spoke to the needs of our educators, and I think this book does just that. I also wanted to provide a list of resources that I have personally researched or used that a teacher can at least try. Listed below are some resources that you can turn to if you are experiencing anxiety or have experienced a traumatic event in the classroom.

- American Psychiatric Association
  https://www.psychiatry.org/patients-families/anxiety-disorders
- National Alliance on Mental Health
  https://nami.org/Learn-More/Mental-Health-Conditions/Anxiety-Disorders

Better Help is an online counseling service that offers access to licensed, trained, experienced, and accredited psychologists (PhD / PsyD), marriage and family therapists (LMFT), clinical social workers (LCSW / LMSW), and board licensed professional counselors (LPC). All of the Better Help counselors have been qualified and certified by their state's professional board after successfully completing the necessary education, exams, training, and practice. While their experience, expertise, and background vary, they all possess at least 3 years and 2,000 hours of hands-on experience.

Through this book, Better help is offering **one month of free counseling services** to anyone that needs it. Please click on the following link to get started with your healing today!

https://www.betterhelp.com/jcs/

The Whole Adventure
Health Coaching for Teachers

The Whole Adventure: Health Coaching for Teachers offers private coaching programs and a monthly membership program with the goal of helping teachers maintain their wellness during a demanding school year. Work-life balance, stress management, and self-care are all subjects covered to help teachers overcome burnout for good and stay in the career they love long-term. Learn more at thewholeadventurecoaching.com

Now, these are just a few resources that I looked into when I got hurt. The first person you should contact if you are having severe issues is your primary care physician. They should also be able to provide you with a list of resources in your area. I encourage you to seek out some sort of assistance and don't try to do this on your own. Anxiety is real. It is something that happens to all of us. Sometimes it comes in short sessions, while other times it lingers like the smell of a dead animal. Whatever your situation is, seek help! Find a support system, go to your local church or go see your doctor.

On a positive note, you are worthy! Teachers are the foundation of the educational system and your students need you! But they need you healthy, whole, and able to handle the multitude of situations we are put in on a daily basis. Don't let anxiety rule your life. Don't let it steal your joy. Don't let it take away your dreams! You are more than your anxiety. You are more than what is happening! Now repeat these daily:

I AM MORE!

I AM WORTHY!

I AM SPECIAL!

I AM BLESSED!

I AM MORE THAN MY ANXIETY!

References

Anxiety. 2019. In *Merriam-Webster.com*. Retrieved September 7, 2019, from https://www.merriam-webster.com/dictionary/anxiety

Index

Anxiety, 2, 6, 7, 9, 10, 14, 18, 62, 66, 71, 73, 75
Better Help, 72
Panic Attacks, 2, 10
Self-care, 2, 27, 62
Teacher 1 Interview, 18
Teacher 2 Interview, 35
Teacher 3 Interview, 46
The Whole Adventure: Health Coaching, 73
Trauma, 2, 53

CPSIA information can be obtained
at www.ICGtesting.com
Printed in the USA
LVHW111333271019
635469LV00001B/111/P

9 780359 918195